The Flower and the Plough

The Flower and the Plough

Love poems by Rachel Piercey

Illustrations by Emma Wright

THE EMMA PRESS

THE EMMA PRESS

First published in Great Britain in 2013
by the Emma Press Ltd

Reprinted in 2015

Poems copyright © Rachel Piercey 2013
Illustrations copyright © Emma Wright 2013

ISBN 978-0-9574596-0-1

A CIP catalogue record of this book
is available from the British Library.

Printed and bound in Great Britain
by Letterworks Ltd, Reading.

theemmapress.com
queries@theemmapress.com

For our parents

Nigel & Kate
David & Mai

Contents

How it works

Ye gods! Annihilate but space and time
And make two lovers happy. Pope

To this I would add: politics;
Your histories, sexual and romantic;
And generally the things that make you tick.

Family tree

Dispersed now in countless
                    bellies of worms

    one mother
        far back as mothers go
    cranks a wheel.

Doesn't know how it turns
cogs locking

        unlocking
through hundreds of years

                        to me

        and you meets me.

My trajectory smacks
                of the inevitable

                slipping sometimes
and sometimes getting
                        caught.

What if you're the slipping kind
        not the catching?

                        What if you're the catching kind?

An old man and woman stand
                        a long way back

        brandishing levers.

When I grew up I got Catullus

A version of Catullus V

Let us live, my _________, and let us love,
and ignore the bores who prose about us
growing up and out of lust!
The sun will always roll around the globe,
but the hours we can wrest to roll
together round the bed are numbered.

So give me a thousand kisses, then another hundred,
and another thousand, and another hundred,
and talk about us till our friends stop asking
and leave your job and move where mine is –
I've got you a diamond and a puppy
and we'll name our children while we walk it,
and we'll list the countries we want to visit
and book for next year and the one after,
and insist we're both invited to parties
and disgust all the guests with our plus-one ardour…

Oh kiss me all the way to the tattoo parlour!
And print us with proof: a pair of sparrows
bearing our initials. With our arms together,
they fly in the same air, and no one
can erase the song they share.

Sleepless night

Three a.m., in bed,
and though the lamp's neck
is twisted back

the light's still harsh,
stripping my fictions
of red lips and composure

right back to character
as first conceived:
a few adjectives

before they're fleshed out,
sketching me
in a single moment –

happy…incautious…amazed…
words that will never
see the light of day.

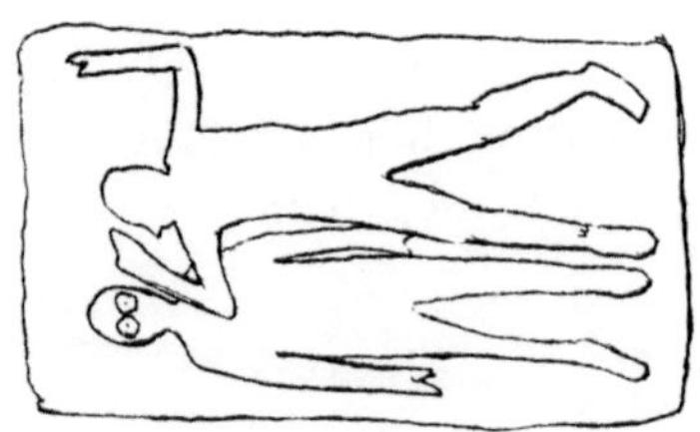

Make it up to you

Having left the girl
waiting by the phone

(after promising to call,
then becoming

too drunk to remember
his intentions)

the only acceptable
form of repentance

was a love poem.
He didn't know her well,

but she had good legs
and he had the blue eyes

that always get 'yes'.
This is how it went:

Meeting you that night,
learning your name,
was a hundred bites
of the sweetest apple.
Nothing tastes the same,
even water is dulled.

He didn't love her
and she didn't love him

but for all that, surely
it was a love poem.

It'll be me again

In cells,
   water is compelled
      to level each side
         of a membrane.

We're here at all
   because heat
      hitches with air
         to smooth out cool.

And the one
   who cares more
      will have all their
         extravagance drawn out.

Bonfire

I have felled
all the trees in my wood
to keep you going,

thrown old faithfuls
and flimsy, startled
saplings into your

hot ears and come-
to-bed mouth.
Then all that was left

was the pointy scent
of gum
and the bellow of an oak.

So I hacked off my hair
with barely
a second thought,

and both ears
were carelessly slung in,
then my thumbs

with their crucial
opposability.
I've got my toes lined up

and my unaccountable hips
and my knees
are ready too,

so please
give me more
of your particular brand

of alchemy.
Because when you temper
scraps into treasure

I think it's worth it,
and when you
spit out glass

though you only got sand
I think it's worth it.
Because I could

spot you
a mile away
on any frightening night

and when I got there
you'd soften me.
Because I hope

that when I'm down
to just my heart in the open air
you'll keep it warm.

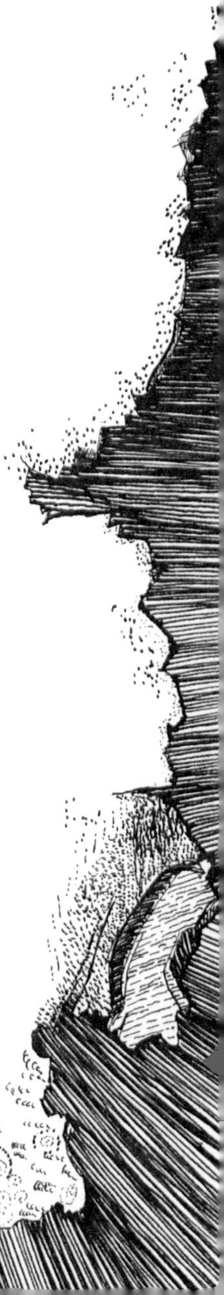

Brief encounter

You and me, two close points
on the concourse, and the train
a magnetic third, drawing you

out of my arms. You move
off, dragging our three sides
through narrowing scalene

towards a single line. Waving,
diminishing, you slip into the train,
and your combined points pull away.

When I grew up I got Catullus (II)

A version of Catullus XI

_____ and _____, companions of _____,
whether you go to find yourself in India,
or lose yourself on a beach at Full Moon,
whether you skim coolly off-piste
down some chic Alp –

wherever you are, you carefree lot,
happy to court the envy of the gods,
perhaps you could take back with you
a tart message for my girl:

I couldn't care less if she messes around.
She has my blessing for all three hundred
of her 'friends', whom she snares like a huntress –
breaking their horns to mount on her wall.

Just don't let her count on my love, like before.
It's her fault it lies in the dust.
The slightest touch from a passing plough
is too much for the flower.

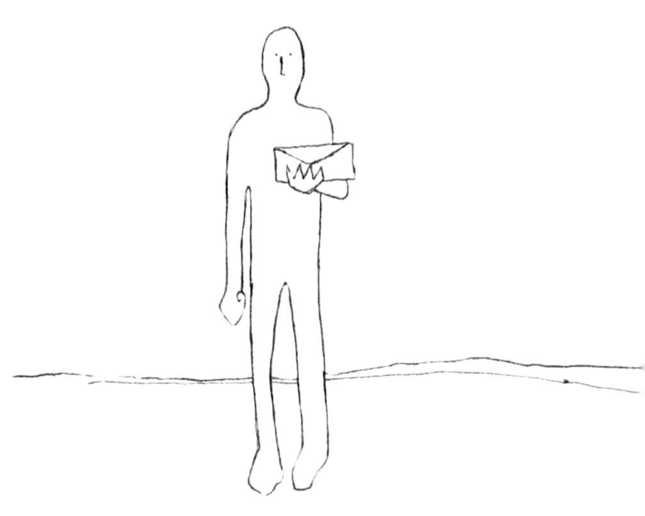

Sea bed

Every sound is pressed out,
every ghost of light.
My miles of skin

feel each force pack it tight.
Only the cusk eel
and the goblin shark

scuff impassively against me,
half-suspended themselves.
I remember one

whose arm smashed me
whose fluke raked through me
who split my heart and held it.

After she'd gone

One insidious
pinkish parabola, clinging
to the rim of a glass.

I thought she was gone,
I was safe from hair pins,
tampons, ringed horoscopes.

I binned her clothes.
I shook out the flowers
in the Yellow Pages

by the list of plumbers.
Now there's one more chance
to press my lips to hers.

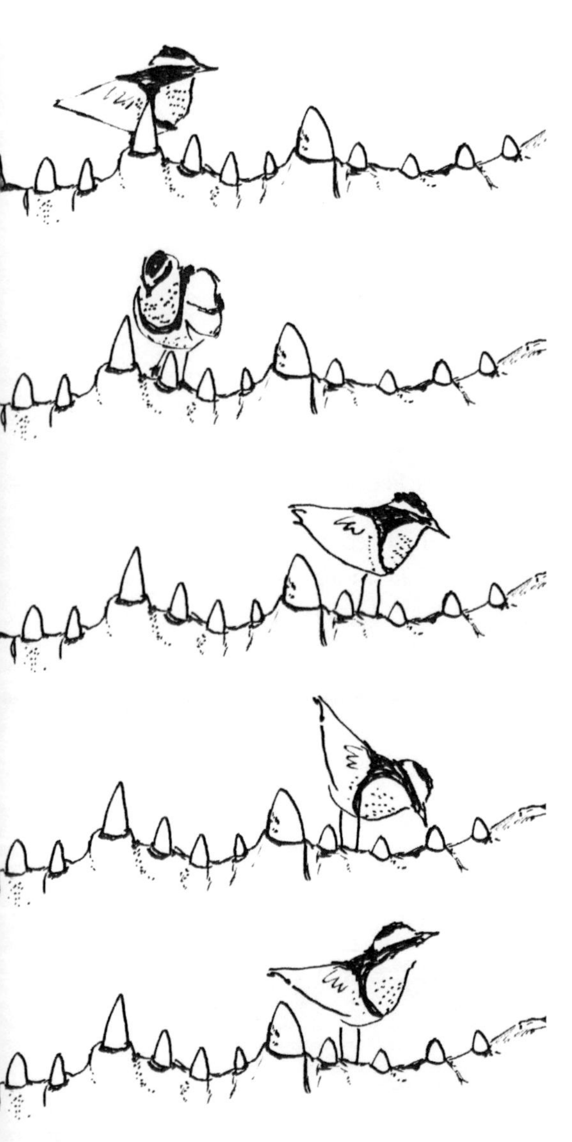

Symbiosis

The Egyptian plover takes for his lover
the Nile crocodile. An unlikely pairing,
feathers with scales, finicking wade with
splayed legs, but she welcomes him wet-eyed
and wide-jawed. He hops within and tenderly
plucks leeches from her gums, so light on her
tongue that each deft step is barely felt
as surviving shifts into caress.

He knows from observation the snap
of tessellating maw round prey,
and once saw his love rip shreds from a giraffe;
when he waded out the river ran red.
But they share four-chambered hearts which beat in time
and he eats at the table of her smile.

LOVE YOU SWEET LESBIA

About the poet

Rachel Piercey is a former editor at *The Cadaverine* magazine and a current editor at the Emma Press. She studied English Literature at St Hugh's College, Oxford, where she won the Newdigate Prize in 2008. Her poems have appeared in various journals and magazines including *Magma, Butcher's Dog* and *The Rialto*. *The Flower and the Plough* is her first pamphlet; her second, *Rivers Wanted* (2014), is also published by the Emma Press.

About the illustrator

Emma Wright studied Classics at Brasenose College, Oxford. She worked in ebook production at Orion Publishing Group before leaving to set up the Emma Press in 2012. In 2015 she was awarded a grant from Arts Council England to run a poetry tour for children. She lives in Birmingham.

Rachel and Emma were the only students in their A-level Latin class, where they became firm friends.

Also from the Emma Press

RASPBERRIES FOR THE FERRY, *by Andrew Wynn Owen*
ISBN: 978 0 9574596 5 6 – PRICE: £6.50

Andrew Wynn Owen dazzles in his debut pamphlet, whisking the reader up with his infectious rhythms and lively sensuality.

IKHDA, BY IKHDA, *by Ikhda Ayuning Maharsi*
ISBN: 978 0 9574596 6 3 – PRICE: £6.50

Reading this book is like being splashed with freezing water and showered with popping candy and wild roses.

OILS, *by Stephen Sexton*
ISBN: 978 1 910139 03 5 – PRICE: £6.50

Belfast poet Stephen Sexton evokes melancholy and a strange kind of romance throughout his brilliant debut pamphlet.

RIVERS WANTED, *by Rachel Piercey*
ISBN: 978 1 910139 04 2 – PRICE: £6.50

Rachel Piercey charms and disturbs in this frequently heart-breaking collection about love, identity and home.

MYRTLE, *by Ruth Wiggins*
ISBN: 978 1 910139 12 7 – PRICE: £6.50

Ruth Wiggins celebrates the primal forces of nature and the human heart in her heady debut, which is full of dry humour and wisdom.

THE EMMA PRESS

small press, big dreams

The Emma Press is an independent publisher dedicated to producing beautiful, thought-provoking books. It was founded in 2012 by Emma Wright in Winnersh, UK, and is now based in Birmingham. The Emma Press was shortlisted for the Michael Marks Award for Poetry Pamphlet Publishers in both 2014 and 2015.

In July-November 2015 we travelled around the country with 'Myths and Monsters', a poetry tour aimed at children aged 8+. This was made possible with a grant from Grants for the Arts, supported using public funding by the National Lottery through Arts Council England.

Our publishing programme features a mixture of themed poetry anthologies and single-author pamphlets, with an ongoing engagement with the works of the Roman poet Ovid. We publish books which excite us and are often on the lookout for new writing.

Sign up to the monthly Emma Press newsletter to hear about our events, publications and upcoming calls for submissions. Our books are available to buy from our online shop, as well as to order or buy from bookshops.

http://theemmapress.com
http://emmavalleypress.blogspot.co.uk/